SOUL DRIVEN POETRY

by

Rita Scribe

Table of Contents

Soul Driven Poetry 1
   About the Author 5
   Acknowledgements 7
   Romance 8
      Coy Love 9
      Coy Flame Requires 12
      Almost Like a Secret 15
      My Love Says 16
      Speak 17
      Intertwined 19
      Think of Your Love 21
   The Journey that is Me and Mine 24
      Roller Coaster 25
      Struggling woman 27
      Pressures 31
      Farewell Family Feud 37
      Wrong, or Right? 42
      Tomorrow Road 44
      Why Shed Tears? 46
      Forever Growing and Re-growing 49
      Try 54

Hero's Tale 57
    The Festival of Red..58
    Silence..60
    Fire Rescued 61
    Just Keep Swimming 64
    White Coats and Scrubs......................................65
The Cards...66
    Kings..67
    Queens 69
    Jacks...71
    Aces 73
Nature 75
    Mother As A Whole...76
    Good 79
    Evil...81
    Candy-Yam..83
    Roses 85
    Coals to Crystals 87
    Morning Summer Breeze.....................................89
    Busy Bee 90
    Baby 92

About the Author

Rita Scribe is an earthy, out-of-the-box creative thinker and writer. Scribe enjoys spending time outdoors surrounded by nature, her children and husband, and animals. She immerses herself in the arts from poetry to children's books to painting to photography to even music and dancing. Residing within southern Louisiana, she grew up grasping firm roots of southern hospitality and manners. Coming from a large military family that split and became even larger at a young age, she had to learn to overcome new challenges and difficulties. Her poetry takes you on an adventure through love and romance; the life of her family and her own emotional journey from adolescent to motherhood; heroes of war and within the community; the different face cards that mask people; and the different aspects of nature. With years of writing and experience in her youthful late twenties, she has accumulated many books awaiting to be published.

Acknowledgements

I would like to, firstly, thank my husband for the support he has given me and the inspiration for some of my written work. I, also, wish to give gratitude towards my family for influencing my life and poetry, and thank you for sharing your opinions and honesty. A special thanks to Mrs. Veazey, my once high school English teacher, for truly believing in me and inspiring me to pursue my creative writing. A thank you to my father for showing me that it is never to late to accomplish your goals and dreams. Thank you all that have helped me and believed in me.

Romance

Coy Love

No need to play shy,

For your smile has caught my eye

I know not shame,

For my heart sparks with a flame.

Need not for modesty,

For I speak with honesty.

Shaky hands and beads of sweat,

For we have only just met.

Why coy you play?

My shining sun ray.

There are no greater feats,

When our hearts as one beats.

Why so coy pray tell,

When in love so deeply we fell?

Any words you wish to hear,

I shall whisper in your ear.

Any touch or embrace,

I shall gladly give with grace.

Before death takes my pride,

Say yes to be my bride.

Your beauty lights the room,

Even if I were entombed.

Your eyes sparkle like stars,

As dazzling as the night sky.

Give me what I require,

To forever burn this fire.

Coy love, no more be shy,

I wait for your reply.

Coy Flame Requires

All we have is time,

And coy is no crime.

If love me like you say,

Then I am very gay.

And yes, we may wither,

But I ask to come hither,

Only if you show me

What and who you can really be.

I do not love ordinary.

My heart belongs to extraordinary.

So, give me a real man,

Or you may never hold my hand.

My passion runs as yours,

But I'm not sure which course.

If flickers like a flame,

Back and forth untamed.

I do not trust what I do not know.

I will ponder a while though.

I could spend a thousand years wandering alone

Just waiting until the day you've shown,

How well I can trust,

Since I feel I must.

If you can warm my heart,

Then we shall never part.

If you can melt the ice,

Then I will be forever nice.

I will no more be coy,

If shown I'm no toy.

Kindness I require,

Or I shall retire.

My flame shall forever burn,

Whether my love for you has a turn.

You've said much about my beauty,

But there is a lot more to me.

I hope you can still my flame,

And never let me walk with shame.

Do not make me cry.

This is my reply.

Almost Like a Secret

My heart is like a flame,

Which burns hot as it flickers.

My heart is like a summer day,

That grows warmer every minute.

My heart is like an ocean,

That is deep and everlasting.

My heart is like a cloud,

Which is moist and always growing.

My heart is like all these things,

With no one ever knowing.

My Love Says

My heart flutters when I behold

The hand of my love as I grow old;

The children I made with my love;

The eyes that say forever and ever;

The times we held close when push comes to shove;

When he said, "I could find no better.

Our hearts beat as one,

You are my family, my angel, my shining sun."

Speak

The butterflies flutter

The drums speed up

Vibrations like thunder

A love-sick pup.

I tremble and shudder

Unable to move

Words are in stutter

With so much to prove

Melting like butter,

Red as a tomato,

Standing like a putter,

How far can I go?

Like pheromones in a cutter,

Slicing through the air,

Shift and sputter,

Sniffing the sweet flare.

Drowning out the clutter,

Concentrate on the task,

I start to mutter

My sweet nothings at last.

Intertwined

The love and surprise

Your lovers eyes

The hope, the excitement

Your loves commitment

Your dreams and goals

Your intertwined souls

Your plans for the future

Your hearts together suture

To grow grey and old

To learn to be bold

To feel your own heart

To not be torn apart

To dance and sing

To wear a wedding ring

To be intertwined

Your forever mine.

Think of Your Love

Think of your love

That was sent from above

Yes, you may fight much

But you melt by his touch

Being held in his arms

You feel save from harm

He wishes for nothing more,

But to love and adore.

He wants to protect you from the world,

Because you are his shining pearl.

You become the best of friends,

And you love till the end.

And you love one another,

Like sister, like brother.

Yes, he is over protective,

And he is overly jealous.

Think of you love,

That was sent from above

Yes, you may fight much,

But you melt by his touch.

Being held in his arms,

You feel save from harm.

He wishes for nothing more,

But to love and adore.

He worries about you,

And doesn't know what to do.

He holds you close,

And holds you tight,

Throughout the day,

And the night,

To make sure you are safe

And secure.

He loves you,

Loves you forever more.

The Journey that is Me and Mine

Roller Coaster

I am a roller coaster,

But not a wooden one.

I am a steel roller coaster,

Built with loops, and turns, and spins,

Filled with circles, and twists, and bends,

With lifts, and drops,

With slow starts and sudden stops,

With quick beginnings and drawn out ends,

That brakes and mends,

That paint and metal starts its tinges,

Made with bolts and screws and hinges.

My mechanics may be complicated,

But once learned, easily navigated.

I am a roller coaster.

I can make you sick,

But am a thrill ride you won't forget.

To feel free, thrilling, and clear,

But caged, secure, and filled with fear.

I end at the start,

And as I depart,

I never know the time efficiency,

For every ride is different for me.

I am a roller coaster.

Struggling woman

She had a hard-happy life

The hard times she fought through made her smarter.

She became wiser and brighter.

She had a hard-happy life

She was one of seven and very poor.

Three youngest went to the orphanage and left the

other four.

She had a hard-happy life,

She worked, made money, and broke them free.

Throughout her life she paid a fee.

She had a hard-happy life.

The years went by and still poor.

Some family died and saw them no more.

She had a hard-happy life.

The years kept going and it was always tough.

She married and wiped off the scuff.

She had a hard-happy life.

They were happy and poor,

And she had four.

She had a hard-happy life.

Drinking away her pain,

Living life in vain.

She had a hard-happy life.

She found God and peace,

And her drinking began to cease.

She had a hard-happy life.

Her children grew up poor, but bright.

She tried to do what was right.

She had a hard-happy life.

Her children had children,

And she tried to live without sin.

She had a hard-happy life.

She became ill,

And prayed for God to heal.

She had a hard-happy life.

She broke her back and began to die.

Her whole family hurt and began to cry.

She had a hard-happy life.

She went with God she trusts.

She had a legacy, and that was all of us.

Pressures

I break under the pressure,

It leans upon me until I snap.

Yes, I can bare a lot,

But not enough to last.

"You should do this."

Yeah you think so" I reply

Yeah, it would be good for you"

So, I comply

When things I should do are said,

I've never done before.

I hate changes and to change,

But unfortunately, it happens every day.

I never really like the outcome.

I don't really like the feel.

Change is not for me

And I ceast to be real.

Maybe the dreamworld I enter

Is part of my weariness,

Because I know I know, I can't do this.

But I still try to hold the weight.

And it weighs me down more and more

"oh, why do I do this?"

I know I cannot endure.

And still I carry it.

Growing weak and weaker

Shaking begin in the legs

Then to the back

And then that is when,

I begin to crack.

"It has already been done."

And now growing sick

I think "oh what have I done?"

"Why do I do this?"

My bones begin to fracture

And I start to bend

One more "Oh, I like"

And I start to give in.

One more "Oh, I like"

Adding one more weight.

I cannot take it anymore!

And then I snap, and break!

"Ok, ok I like it!"

I have given in!

Secretly, I still don't like it,

But quiet as can be,

Because I know down inside,

This is not for me.

This was not part of my plan,

And is something new.

I fear this unreal feel

Because it's something new.

I fear the weight.

I fear the change.

I fear that I don't have the strength,

But still I try to pull through.

I let the pressure build.

And even after I try,

To take the weight and put it aside,

It builds back up again.

Stop the rocks from forming.

Stop the stones from building.

I can't stop the rocks from forming.

I can't stop the stones from building,

But I could keep trying.

And stop the denying.

That I have the strength,

Because we all do.

And what do I need to do.

I wish I could have said,

"No, I don't like these things,

And these things I do.

I am unique like you,

And have things I like to do.

But some things are only to try once,

And others never to try at all.

It never hurts to try

But some only to try once

And do not weigh it on me

To try it every day.

I am not like my friends,

Who follow all the trends.

I do not know fashion, jewelry, or makeup,

But I don't mind doing work.

I don't know about nails,

And do not like to tan.

But with the pressure,

I must try it once.

I might break under the pressure.

It may lean upon me until I snap.

Yes, I can bare a lot,

But not enough to last.

Farewell Family Feud

I never want to be,

In their minds at all.

I do not want to see,

When it is their final fall

I did not ever feel,

Like I was really real.

I nurtured their every need,

And gave them their every desire.

I did not ever heed,

And they managed to put out my fire.

I wished for the end,

Because my holes would never mend.

Cared and gave, I did.

Mother, I became,

And mother became the kid.

Then I was tame.

I wanted to get away,

Like I still do today.

Whine and complained,

My children always did.

Every night it rained,

And I wanted to be rid.

I felt lonely and alone,

Like I was all on my own.

Used and abused, they continued.

They hurt and wounded me.

I tried to change my mood,

But by then I could not see.

I was blinded to the changes they made.

And I hid all in the shade.

I was lost,

Confused and bruised,

My freedom is cost,

And I was used.

I faked happiness,

And became senseless.

I was shown,

What was happening.

Now, I've grown,

And moving out happily.

I cannot pretend anymore.

And I will not settle the uneven score.

It was never fair,

And it was not right.

They did not care,

And now I fight.

I used to just conform,

With their evil mourn.

But I have found love and happiness,

And they hate it passionately.

I will live a life of bliss,

And they will live miserably.

Now I will leave,

Forever for all the times they disowned me.

Unappreciative and greedy,

Immature babies,

Selfish and needy,

Backstabbing shadies,

Good reddens, farewell.

I will see you all in hell.

Wrong, or Right?

With content and distain

I sit with unending pain

To never say what I wish to say

For I am nothing more than a slave

With love and understanding

I comfort without demanding

To be nurtured like the other

For I am not the mother.

With hope and desire

I pray with all avenging fire

To set forth my wrath of vengeance

For I am nemesis

With sorrow and resolute

I stand with solitude

To step forth away from this

For I am more than a child not missed

With years of knowledge and experience

I walk my own footsteps

To treat other without cruel intention

For I am a person

Tomorrow Road

To feel lost and hopeless

Down the broken road

Your path a mess

To feel the heavy load

The burdens are rough

The road is long

But they will make you tough

And you will grow strong.

It seems never ending

You hardly see light

You are always defending

Against the cold night.

Soon they say

Your light will come

It will happen someday

You deserve some.

Maybe tomorrow

Tomorrow you pray

With tears of sorrow

Tomorrow's the day

Why Shed Tears?

Yesterday I wept tears of shame

Last week I wept tears of pain

Last month I wept tears of happiness

Last year I wept tears for someone I miss

Yesterday I cried for my action

Last week I cried for my reaction

Last month I cried for my selfishness

Last year I cried for my relentlessness.

Yesterday I wept because of my pride

Last week I wept because of my side

Last month I wept because of my heart.

Last year I wept because of my smart.

Yesterday I cried because a gift.

Last week I cried because a lift.

Last month I cried because a love in my life

Last year I cried because a question to be my wife.

Yesterday my tears fell for a far away friend.

Last week my tears fell for a fight not mend.

Last month my tears fell for a passed animal.

Last year my tears fell for a love one's burial.

Yesterday I wept tears of sorrow.

Last week I wept tears for tomorrow.

Last month I wept tears of joy

Last year I wept tears for Roy.

Tears are wept for different things.

A joke, a cut or a ring.

Tears are wept for all emotions,

Anger, pain, joy, and demotion.

Tears are tears and nothing more

Let it rain, let it pour,

Tears are tears, and nothing change

Let it pour, let it rain.

Forever Growing and Re-growing

To love the feeling

To love the knowledge

To love the growing

To love the child

To love thinking about the future

Your baby's crib

Your baby's first laugh

Your baby's eyes

Your baby's first bath

What to buy?

What to name?

IS it a boy?

Or is it a dame?

Can't wait to see

Can't wait to grow

That huge belly

So, everyone knows

Smiling bright

Smiling big

Everyone drinks to the baby

But you don't take a swig.

You do everything right

You do nothing wrong,

But unexpectedly,

You begin to see,

Crimson red that starts to leak,

Pains on all sides,

And you begin to worry,

But you calm yourself down,

Because you know it can't be.

But you hurt so you want to be sure.

You wait and wait and wait some more.

Then the doctors come in,

And you don't really worry,

They don't seem bothered

Nor in a scurry

Than after done

They turn to you and say

"IT seems like you're having a…"

And everything goes grey.

Everything that was so joyous, happy, and gay.

The flood comes, and your ears go red

Your world crashes,

And your soul is dead.

Why did it happen?

What did you do?

You don't want to speak

And you cannot talk

Waiting forever, stunned by shock,

It doesn't matter, justified or not.

You blame yourself,

And nothings forgot.

Time passes,

And life goes on

Another seed sprouts

And joy envelopes

Once again you are filled with hope

Soon you see the picture

You feel a kick

You taste new things,

Your smell is heightened

You hear the precious screams

And tears fill your eyes

How blessed you are,

To have grown this life inside.

Try

Every day I try,

Try to be a good mother,

Try to be a good friend,

Try to be happy,

Try to make other happy.

Every day I try,

I try to listen,

I try to teach,

I try to learn,

I try to preach.

Every day I try,

Try something new,

Try to remember the past,

Try to find the truth,

Try to be truthful.

Every day I try,

I try to live,

I try to love,

I try to give,

I try to thank God above.

Hero's Tale

The Festival of Red

All I see is red,

Red bodies dancing in my head,

Playing music with the barrels,

And shooting fireworks from the Aerials.

My brothers and my friends

With wholes they'll never mend.

The smell of a feast of beast,

But this is not my feast.

Singing songs sweet of sweat,

The music deafening,

The bodies weary,

The feast prepared,

But who will eat?

I don't care.

My body like lead.

Those around asleep like dead.

The fireworks' sound bleeds my ears,

Now, I can barely hear.

But the music from the barrels,

Rang loud and quick in the head of Darrel's.

Silence

Secretly swimming,

Deep below the ocean blue,

Turbine spines iron screw.

Fire Rescued

Alarm alerts all.

Black smoke fills the room.

Calm, stay calm.

Door is hot too.

Evacuate, but there is no escape.

Fear sets in.

Glass breaks.

Help, please help.

I'm here to help you.

Just hold my hand.

Keep close.

Lit up rooms,

Melting knobs,

No space left neglected.

Obliterating all,

Protected by the person in the suit.

Question not, they have been trained what to do.

Raging, roaring flames surround.

Sirens wail just outside.

Trusting life and limb.

Unwilling to give up.

Victory at last.

Water rushes taming the flames

Xerostomia, hypoxemia,

Zombification all need treatment.

Just Keep Swimming

Laughing, I feel the curves of her waves.

Splishing and Splashing I count my saves.

Can't go no more.

I start to feel sore.

Beneath her bosom she takes her slaves.

White Coats and Scrubs

Some wear white coats

And others wear scrubs.

Vigorously trying to solve the puzzle

Efficiently testing for pieces uncovered.

Sticking needles,

And filling syringes,

Noting changes,

Deciphering images,

Logging hours,

Operating surgeries,

Scrubs and Surgeons work as a team.

Saving a life when they can.

Everyone wins.

Sometimes they lose.

Scribe / Soul Driven Poetry / 66

The Cards

Kings

Royal Kings,

Kings of Flush

Hearts of Kings,

Kings that crush.

Humble Kings,

Kings of Spades,

Angry Kings,

Kings in graves.

English Kings

King of old,

New Kings,

Kings so bold,

Proud Kings

Kings of jewels,

Glutton Kings,

Kings of fools.

Queens

Queen Bees,

Queen Ants,

Queen of Italy,

Queen of France,

Queen of hearts,

Queen of Spades,

Queen of the arts,

Queen of the trades,

Queen of divas,

Queen of drag,

Queen of shivas,

Queen of rags,

Queen of soul,

Queen of clubs,

Queen of rock and roll,

Queen of cherubs.

Jacks

My Jack of hearts

My Jack of trades

My Jack of diamonds

My Jack of spades

My Jack be nimble

My Jack is quick

My Jack be kind

My Jack of brick

My Jack is strong

My Jack is cunny

My Jack is bright

MY Jack is funny

MY hi Jack

My low Jack

My hungry Jack

My slap Jack

Aces

The Ace of dice

The Ace of dominos,

The Ace that flies,

The Ace of Astros,

The golfers Ace,

The Ace at tennis,

Ace of Base,

The Ace at Stennis,

Ace of cards,

Ace in the hole,

Ace of hearts,

Ace as low,

Aces high,

Aces spades,

Ace of my eye,

Ace of trades.

Nature

Mother As A Whole

Loving the life lived by I;

You gave me the tears that I cry.

They match your tears from the sky.

You are chooser of if I live or die.

You are the best Mother in the entire world.

This world is yours and you are it.

Working hard, knowing you can't quit.

Fixing, renewing with every hit.

No time to sleep, stop, or sit.

You are the hardest worker for the entire world.

The wind is your music,

The trees sway to the tune of rhythmic,

The bodies of water dance in mimic,

The creatures dance with whom they pick.

Your creations dance for you all over the world.

Beautiful trees

Brown, Orange, yellow, green leaves,

Everyone sees,

All, of your beauties.

You are beautiful all around the world.

You are the best,

Work harder than the rest.

Creatures dance with zest.

Your creations are the prettiest.

You are the world, and Mother Earth is your name.

Good

The good filled with love, peace, and harmony.

You can see the happy, the just, and the beauty.

So hard to be.

So hard to come by.

Can you see past the corrupt to see the good?

I just sigh,

I wish everyone could.

Like a new born baby,

Like a mother giving birth,

Like a blossoming daisy,

Like Mother Earth,

Like a baby's first laugh,

Like a sunny day,

Like a new calf,

Like a kind word to say.

Find the inner beauty to find peace,

And once you've found that, you have found the

Golden Fleece.

Evil

The evil filled with hate, violence, and calamity.

You can see the cruel, the corrupt, and the ugly.

So easy to be.

So easy to become.

Can you see through the just to see the evil?

I just hum,

I pity the hateful.

Like a poisonous snake,

Like a venomous bite,

Like a deadly lake,

Like a brutal fight,

Like a baby's death,

Like a dark day,

Like a teenager on meth,

Like a cruel word to say.

Find the hideousness in yourself to find hate,

And once you've done that you've shut the gate.

Candy-Yam

My sweet Candy-yam

Lovely as ever

As sweet as the brown sugar

The aroma of your presence never to be compared.

Home grown wild beauty

Firmly rooted and ripe with ambition

With rich nutrition

The roots of your existence shown by how well you

grow.

Made fresh from natures seed

Blended with the best mixtures

Baked with love and tenderness

The perfection that is you.

Roses

Your thorns may prick,

But your spirit blooms.

Your soft petals are silky and slick,

And you exert alluring perfumes.

In all colors you glow,

From bright to gloomy.

In all areas you grow,

From root to outer beauty.

Your stem matures intricately,

And your aroma remains sweet,

Your aptitude to amaze decoratively,

And your longevity is a treat.

Your prickles are there to protect,

Your beauty and soul that is delicate.

Coals to Crystals

The coal that burns with energy,

May be pressured by mentality.

Built by so much chemistry,

Coal has its own personality.

Keep bringing the excessive heat,

Until the day they meet.

Here Coal and Crystal greet,

And neither retreat.

This Crystal's hardness beyond compare,

With beauty and purity that is so rare.

Handled with exquisite care,

The quality unfound elsewhere.

The hardest of Coal,

Of yet to behold,

Helped form the hard Crystal mold,

To never be sold.

Morning Summer Breeze

In the morning,

It blows soft and slow,

Just once or twice,

To let everyone know,

It is nice outside,

Feel the wind flow,

Summer head does not win,

Summer breeze does blow.

Busy Bee

The sun shines bright,

Warmth encasing me,

My wings flutter fast,

I'm a buzzing bee.

Flower to flower,

All day I fly,

Minding my business,

As others go by.

I do my part.

I do my best.

I work hard.

I do not rest.

The day is bright.

The day is sunny.

My work brings beauty.

My work makes honey.

Baby

A baby,

Beautiful child.

Cooing delightfully,

Delicate, eager,

Pure love starts with the birth of a baby.

www.ingramcontent.com/pod-product-compliance
Lightning Source LLC
Chambersburg PA
CBHW030442220526
45464CB00006B/2387